The After Life

Synopsis and presentation of the feature film project and TV show.

DiaryUnlimited.com

The After Life was originally published in 2012 by The Edge Press (UK) and DiaryUnlimited (U.S.). AnotherClip.com

Published as a DiaryUnlimited.com paperback by The Edge Press and Mnemonics Publishing, an imprint of Global Edge Mnemonics LLC, New York

ISBN 978-0-9526607-3-6

Printed in the USA

www.DiaryUnlimited.com

www.VirtualAlien.net

www.AnotherClip.com

Design and Layout by Tom Norwood

The After Life

A film and TV show

Synopsis

Synopsis and presentation of the feature film project and TV show.

Two candidates are assembled inside a locked room. The master of ceremony, the TV host, is asking the candidates to sit around a large round table. The candidates are then introduced one by one by the TV host.

Each guest must introduce the person they want to get in touch with in the "after life". The light is then switched off and the show continues in the dark. Each candidate is seen only through a 2D outline in white (Sometimes in colour using 3D). The TV show host is getting in touch with the "after life" and communicates with the candidates the results and in turn they react accordingly.

The light can only be switched on again when the show's episode is over.

Dramatis Personae

Gabriel

Zach

Reverend Piccard
He is in his early sixties. He has a clear and concise voice. He has deep penetrating and hypnotic eyes. He has a very dominant approach when he needs to extract some information from a candidate. He has a great knowledge of human interaction with spiritualism. Reverend Piccard was once a clergyman but left ten years ago to concentrate on researching the "after life".

A TV presenter

Five members of the crew

The three assistants of Reverend Piccard seen at the end

Screenplay

Scene 1: "Into the story"

View of the countryside and the castle where the show is taking place.

The TV show host is narrating the presentation superimposed over the footage.

TV Presenter

Reverend Piccard's favourite motto is "You cannot enjoy life on earth unless you can understand what lies ahead inside the "after life "".

The "after life" is the state of our "being" beyond our earthling life. Once we have crossed the divide to the "afterlife" we can't go back to earth, not in our present "human" form.

There is a way to communicate with the "after life". We can get in touch; we can talk and feel the lost one who transcended to the "after life". It is not easy to reach someone in the "after life". That is why we are all gathered in here tonight; to travel where no one has dared to go: to the "after life".

Scene 2: "The TV Show"

Inside the castle where the show is set

Reverend Piccard

We really need to understand each other here as I do not want any misunderstandings. The experiment we are about to witness here is unique in the history of one man's life. We will enter a zone where you have never been before; a zone where most humans will never go unless they are dead. We are entering a zone known as the "after life".

You will not move from your chair. You will not say anything until requested to do so by myself or the people you are about to meet. We will hold hands and we will bond together until I say otherwise. You will not break this bond at any time! We will hold hands firmly together for the duration of the procession.

We are about to communicate with the "after life". We are about to make contact with what in our earthling life we consider the "dead". But "dead", these people are not! They are inside a different zone. They move on in time and space; where the year 5000 BC meets the year 3000 AD.

We will try to meet someone you have known in the past but are no longer with, someone that you consider "deceased" or "dead". We may be able to but we may be in contact with someone else who met these people and who might be able to tell us what they are doing.

Now it's time for my guests here tonight to tell us a bit about who they are and with whom they wish to contact and connect with in the "after life". You must understand that the encounter will be short. Whatever you have to say and ask must be clear and short.

Scene 3: "Presentation of the candidates"

Zach Intro

Zach

Hi, I'm Zach. I'm from Leicester, England but I live in Southampton.

I'm 24. I'm a car mechanic. My brother died when I was 16 and he was 10. There is so much I want to tell him and I want to know what his life is like.

Gabriel Intro

Gabriel

My name is Gabriel. I'm 30. I'm originally from Dundee, Scotland but I moved to Edinburgh when I was little, then to London. I'm currently unemployed. My mom died when I was 10. Her name is Carla. I'm here because I have a few things I'd like to know about me and her.

Scene 4: "Into the Night"

Reverend Piccard

I believe it's time to commence the procession.

Short pause.

I will ask you both to hold my hands and close this bond that we are about to generate by holding your other hand together.

Short pause.

Are we all set?

I will ask you to shut your eyes and concentrate. You must start thinking very deeply in your head about why you are here: the purpose of this gathering and the precise meaning of your presence here.

Short pause.

Silence! Please now hear the "after life" ...

Scene 5: "The Night"

Pitch black for a few seconds. Then reverse to a black (the elements) on a white background sequence.

Reverend Piccard

Now I want you both to start remembering precisely where you were and when it was the last time you were in contact with your "deceased".

Short pause.

Think carefully about the exact moment in time. Think about the last thing you said to each other. Remember your relatives' voice and what their last few words were.

Short pause.

Now try to remember the face. The way they moved; something about them.

Scene 6: "In the zone 1"

This is a multi-distorted coloured zone with the camera on the candidate's face only. Gabriel and Zach are responding to the people in the "after life".

Q&A 1: Gabriel

Gabriel
Why is it so cold in here?
Short pause.
Who's there?
Who?
What?
Short pause.
It's not right here.
Short pause.
I don't need this! I don't have to be there.
Short pause.
Who touched me? Someone just touched me again!
Short pause.
What? Who's talking? What? There is someone here!
Short pause.
I don't like this. Who are you?
Short pause.
It's all over me! It's squeezing me!
It hurts! Let me go!
What? What are you saying?
What was my mother?

At the end:

Who are you to tell me that my mother deserved it? She didn't deserve to die!

Short pause.

Fuck You! What was that?

His left punch and arm are seen crossing his face and moving out off camera. Cut to Q&A 1 Zach "At the end".

Back on Gabriel

Gabriel
Take this!

Back on Q&A 1 Zach at the end.

Q&A 1: Zach
Is there anyone there?
Short pause.
I can feel something!
Short pause.

What? **Short pause.** No, I'm all alone. **Short pause.** I'm just passing.
Short pause. Who are you? **Short pause.** Do you know my brother Jack? **Short pause.** You met him? **Short pause.** Yes, that's right; he has a large scar over his forehead. **Short pause.** He fell off his bicycle when he was little. **Short pause.** Is he around? **Short pause.** Alive?

He is interrupted by Gabriel

Who's talking here?

Lower underneath his head, a punch and an arm are seen across the screen

Back over the camera
Someone just hit me!

Fucking hell! Who did this?
Lower underneath his head, a punch and an arm are seen across the screen

Back to Zach's face.
Again!

Scene 7: "In the zone 2"

Pitch black for one minute. A fight is being heard.

The sound of the chairs being thrown on the floor is heard. Zach and Gabriel are fighting with each other on the floor. The voice of Reverend Piccard can be heard over.

Stop it! Stop it right now! You are disturbing the dead!
Help! Lights! Lights now! Help!

Scene 8: "Interval"

Interval with full lights

The lights have been switched on. Zach is seen over Gabriel on the floor fighting. Five members of the crew and the TV host are entering the set and along with Reverend Piccard they are trying to split them up.

Reverend Piccard
Stop now! You do not even know each other.
Looking at Gabriel
You thought you were fighting the dead but in fact you were fighting with Zach.

It's crazy! We had a link! We had a link to the "after life" and you broke it! I'm not sure we can get back into it now. Can you please shake each other's hands and apologise then move back behind the table?

Zach and Gabriel are seen shaking hands and apologising to each other with a forced smile.

Reverend Piccard
Can we have some new chairs please?

The five members of the TV crew are removing the broken chairs and are bringing two new chairs.

Reverend Piccard

Now can you please all sit down again and take a deep breath? ***Zach and Gabriel sit down with red faces, slightly bruised. The TV crew and the TV host are leaving the set.***

Try and concentrate! Close your eyes and think! Back in time, back to when you were little, when you were with your deceased.
Concentrate! Try to remember!

Scene 9: "Into the Night 2"

The light is off. It is pitch black for a few seconds.

Reverend Piccard

Remember where you were the last time you spoke with the "dead". What was the last thing the "deceased" said to you? The last thing you said to them!

Scene 10: "In the zone 3"

Reverse sequence black out of white.
Finally getting in contact...

Reverend Piccard
I can feel it! I can feel someone. There is someone there. There are a few people here. Concentrate. Remember! Go deep and deeper than this.

Q&A 2: Gabriel
Gabriel
I feel that there is someone here. Many people are here but I can't see anyone. This is just stupid.
Short pause.

How can you talk to the dead anyway?
Short pause.

Nothing; there is nothing at all. I can't hear anyone.
Short pause.

The TV host is a dangerous crook. What sort of a medium is he? I should have never signed up to this TV show.
Short pause.

I'm nowhere. It's freezing here. I feel like I'm being watched and touched too but I can't see anyone. There is no one.
Short pause.

This is hell! I don't want to talk to my mom anyway. I hate her anyway. I think I've always done it. She's dead and she can stay here. I want to go! I want to get out! Can you hear me?

Q&A 2: Zach

Zach

Can you see me? I can only see some shadows. **Short pause.** Yes, I'm the brother. **Short pause.** Where? **Short pause.** Where "over there"? **Short pause.** But that's his voice! **Short pause.**

Is that you? I can't see you. **Short pause.** You're alive? **Short pause.** Not there? What do you mean? **Short pause.** But you're here... with no face. **Short pause.** I remember. That's why I wanted to see you again, to talk to you. I've missed you so much. **Short pause.**

You knew? **Short pause.** How could you know? **Short pause.** Oh, I'm so glad. I really wanted you to know that I was really, really so sorry. I never pushed the shelves, Darren did. **Short pause.** You knew that too? How did you know?

Short pause. You can see and hear in the past? …And the future? **Short pause.** Why not? **Short pause.** But you're dead now! **Short pause.** You're alive? Not on earth? **Short**

pause. Are you happy here? **Short pause.** Yes, now I'm happy too.

Short pause. I wish I could always be with you. **Short pause.** You have to go now? Why? No, don't go, don't...

Scene 11 "The Final Talk"

Reverend Piccard

Tonight, we have been where only a few have dared to go. Tonight, we have crossed the boundaries of time and space. Tonight, we have entered a zone where no earthling creatures can return.

The "after life" is, as we understand it, a point of no return; an area in space that we can only access through the power of the mind. Nature works in some mysterious ways. It defies the basic principles of physics. The "after life" is yours to conquer and conquer it, you will!

Scene 12: "The Final Zone"

Reverse sequence of the footage of Scotland seen at the beginning.

Scene 13: "The Selection"

The TV presenter is seen superimposed over the footage of hundreds of candidates queuing for an interview with Reverend Piccard and his assistants.

TV Presenter

Anyone can become a candidate in Reverend Piccard's show: "The After Life". Not anyone can make it to the TV show. Candidates are selected from a long list. Members of the public who apply must show some evidence of a lost relation, demonstrate a strong determination to succeed in their quest of knowledge and above all else must be of a strong and sane temperament.

Scene 14: "The Interviews"

The candidates are being interviewed one by one by Reverend Piccard and his three assistants. The interviews never last more than one minute and very often the candidates are requested by Reverend Piccard to leave the room only after a few seconds. The candidates must undergo the interview standing up.

The END

Development

Notes

Intro: "Sequence 1"

1. Images of Scotland/V.O. intro, going up the stairs to a room inside the castle.

Last image: picture of the scene with all the characters around a table.

2. "The TV Show 1": (in full colour) introduction of the two candidates by the TV host around the table inside a castle.

3. Black screen with white silhouettes of the show host and the two candidates entering the "after life". "Sequence W/B 1" The Show host is talking to the dead relatives of candidate N.1 in the show.

4. "Q/A 1" sequence. In the dark, camera on the face of candidate N.1. The face of the candidate N.1 is painted with a fluorescent colour.

5. Back to "the TV Show 2"

6. "Sequence W/B 2": with candidate N.2

7. "Q/A 2" sequence with candidate N.2

8. Back to "the TV Show 3"

9. "Sequence W/B 3": with candidate N.1

10. "Q/A 3" sequence with candidate N.1

11. Back to "the TV Show 4"

12. "Sequence W/B 4": with candidate N.2

13. "Q/A 4" sequence with candidate N.2
14. Final "TV Show 5": Epilogue.

15. Outro: "Sequence 2" same sequence as in the intro but in reverse starting from all the candidates and the show host around the table until the Scottish countryside is seen.

16. "Q/A" sequence: the candidates are answering questions and asking questions to the relatives; each guest in turn.

End Credits

The TV Show

"You cannot enjoy life on earth unless you can understand what lies ahead inside the "after life". "Reverend Piccard

Season 1: 12 episodes

Episode #1: Intro

Selection process of ten candidates; introduction of the show and presentation of the "after life".

Episode #2 - #11

One candidate is introduced to the "after life" whilst the other candidates witness the experience.

Episode #12

The final: summary of the season with interviews of the candidates (with the ones who dared to remain until the end) about their journeys.

The After Life - 2012

www.ingramcontent.com/pod-product-compliance
Lightning Source LLC
LaVergne TN
LVHW050950080826
845145LV00004B/1461

* 9 7 8 0 9 5 2 6 6 0 7 3 6 *